OLD STORIES

Old Stories

Maggie Martin

Copyright © 2014 Maggie Martin

All rights reserved. No part of this book may be used or reproduced in any manner without written permission of the publisher. Please direct inquiries to Niobe Press at niobepress@gmail.com.

ISBN:0615832261
ISBN-13:9780615832265

FOR MY FAMILY

CONTENTS

I

Dirt *5*
I Come From Coal *6*
Grandpa And The Gypsies: A Poem-Story For My Grown-Up Son *7*

II

My Mother's Favorite Song Was *Dancing In The Dark* *17*
Cecelia *18*
Sleep-Over With Aunt Ceil In Her Bedroom At Aunt May's *19*
Tereza And The Unanswered Questions—
Especially the ones about her shoes *20*
Sabato John's Second Wife *22*
201 Oak Street *24*
201 Oak Revisited *25*

III

It Was More Than The Smell Of Lava Soap *29*
Old Women's Shoes *31*
The Final Say *32*

IV

Food That Is More Than Food *35*
Old Stories *37*

I

DIRT

She sits in the tall grass,
Pretends not to smell
The sour smell of water trapped
In bottoms of broken bottles.
Thick, green glass edges
Smoothed by countless summer rains.

She twists a tarnished silver teaspoon
Into the earth still damp and cold
In the afternoon sun.
Lifts up clumps of soil undisturbed
For centuries before her parents breathed her name.
She digs to get dirty.

All over the neighborhood
Sweating women grip
Rough wood handled brushes.
Dip into hot soapy water
In pitted metal buckets
Behind latched kitchen screen doors.

I COME FROM COAL

My ears resound with the sound of coal
Avalanching down the metal chute
Into the basement coal bin
Gleaming blue-black
Common gems
Falling over one another
Loudly piling up and up
As I stood watching
Fearing I'd be swallowed by them
Never to breathe again
My mouth packed tight
With rounded chunks of darkness.

Saved by the shriek of metal
As the chute withdrew
I sucked in a breath
And plunged into the pile with my shovel
While my father fed the furnace
Its mouth gaping
Fiery tongues lashing
Red hot nuggets crackling
Like the fires of hell.

I come from coal
My bones are filled with marrow black
Liquid carbon fills my veins
The legacy of men whose faces never saw the light of day
Whose lungs were filled with pockets filled with dust
Whose hearts beat out a rhythm
As they dug into the earth's jet core.

My mouth tastes of the waiting
The ritual of women who listened for the warning sound
The shattering of the shaft
As they birthed the children, cooked the meals
Pretending not to wait.

GRANDPA AND THE GYPSIES: A POEM-STORY FOR MY GROWN-UP SON

CHAPTER ONE: *MUDTOWN*

Few people in Mudtown were fearless enough
To follow the Gypsies home.
The Gypsy camp sat at the edge of town
Beyond the invisible line
Where everything familiar fell away.
No one there to ask which way to go.

The Gypsies would gather, laugh, drink
Share food cooked over an open fire
And sing.
The Gypsies always sang.
Voices rose with wisps of smoke
Far above the cover of trees alive with summer.
Reached for ancestral routes across the evening sky
To serenade the moon.

Never for a moment did the Gypsies doubt
The power of their songs.
Especially when Sorrow came.
They had no desire to give it a home
More permanent than any they had ever known.
Too busy living each day as if it were the last.
Tomorrow a sickness might strike
Curse come full circle
Business affair go awry.

We have no right to question how the Gypsies lived
Removed from ruts left in the mud by horse-drawn carts
Along the Main Street of Mudtown.
It is important only to believe that they did.

Not a person remains to tell us with certainty
How many winters had burned away in heaps of coal
Hauled from mine shafts
Hidden under Mudtown's houses
When young William, your grandfather,
Perhaps as old as you are now,
Without looking back to see who was watching
Not marking the place he had left behind
Guided by sounds of their laughter and singing
Followed the Gypsies home.

CHAPTER TWO: *THE HORSE*

It has become a familiar sight since our William
Returned from the Gypsy camp
Walking with the horse at his side—
His white shirtsleeves, loosely rolled in the
Crooks of his arms browned by the sun.
Long, elegant fingers of his right hand
Gently interlaced in Beauty's mane,
The color of rich chocolate.
The color of his eyes.

Beauty has no need for reins or saddle
As she and William make their way
Toward the meadow at the top of The Hill
Where she knows she'll run free
Rear up on her hind legs
Pretend to take a nip out of clouds,
Puffy and white, scuttering across the sky.
Nibble at wild grass
Tall enough to bow to summer breezes
On their way to sanctify freshly washed bed sheets
Clinging to clotheslines strung up
In backyards that lead out to alleyways
Muddy as the streets of Mudtown.

They tell stories of how sometimes at night the two,
Side by side, circled in silver-bright moonlight,
Ascend the path to the top of The Hill.
Beauty slows her pace
Bends to listen as William whispers in her ear
Pauses before she answers.

All who have witnessed the scene, young and old,
Swear on their ancestors' souls
They have not been dreaming.

CHAPTER THREE: *THE FATEFUL DAY*

Looking back on that day
Neighbors will remind one another
How mystified they felt
As young William, Beauty at his side,
Walked past them not speaking a word.
He acted as if they had never been born!
Never wished him *Buona Sera* on summer evenings
Sweetened by the scent of Citronella.
Never failed to call out their hellos
Across hedgerows clipped to perfection,
Flourishing despite the heat.
Never teased about falling for a *gypsy girl*
And riding away on his horse forever.

As if while making morning beds,
Tucking sheet corners with precision,
Neighbor-women never listened
Through open, upstairs windows,
Whistling along as he played his cornet.

Born under the Sign of the Fishes
Assured of a tender and generous heart
Youngest son of Sabato John
Whose poor wife, Mary Ann
Died before her dear son could claim her,
William was regarded as a fine young man
By the fathers of Mudtown.
Hovered over, loved by the mothers
As one of their own.

All the more reason to question at the time.
How could he hurt them so?
Walk by
And not answer?

CHAPTER FOUR: *THE LONG WALK*

How could their young William walk
Unaware of crows
Flying one-by-two-by-twenty
Without their raucous cawing,
Blackening branches of maples and oaks
Ready to provide Beauty with shade on her way.

No longer do chicken hawks screech
Dogs howl
Insects scurry between blades of grass
Bees drone in the clover.

No mourning doves *coo, coo* to catch his attention.

Pigeons crouch
Silent in their coops.

Katydids have ceased their constant shrill,
Like the murmur of Mudtown's old ladies
Dressed in black, oblivious to heat and cold
As they caress crystal rosary beads,
Heads lowered.
Babushkas tightly tied beneath their chins
Cover coils of hair
Unfastened no longer
By anyone's fingers except their own.

CHAPTER FIVE: *STRAIGHT AHEAD*

William walked, holding Beauty's mane gently,
As he always did on their way to The Hill.
He took no notice of his neighbors' greetings.

Nor the purple grapes clustered
Among green leaves
Twisted around
Garden arbors.

Nor the prickly pink rosettes
Fleeing front yard trellises
Escaping
Over whitewashed picket fences.

He never heard The Silence
Seep into the mud
Up and down the alleys and
Streets of Mudtown.

No room in his ears for any sound
Other than the fury
In his father's voice.

It was as if his father still stood before him
Forbidding him to buy a horse from the Gypsies,
Suffering from who knows what awful disease.
Dying, no doubt, before the first leaves fall!

CHAPTER SIX: *HARD TO SWALLOW*

William was forced to swallow his father's words,
Like a dose of Castor Oil.
Like the lies told to him by the Gypsies.
Even so he could never hate them.
Never regret the deal he made for Beauty.

He first saw her the day blossoms,
White as angels' wings,
Fell from the Pear Tree, scenting Mudtown's air
Before carpeting the Chapel Yard,
Compelling passers-by to smile.

The day the caravan returned
As it did every spring.
Gypsies waved, paraded their wares,
Welcome once more in Mudtown.
No matter how many useless trinkets they'd sold
Or clucking chickens they'd stolen from backyard gardens
All the years before.

CHAPTER SEVEN: *ALMOST THERE*

And now on this day,
When summer has begun to relinquish its
Grasp on the everyday lives
Of the people of Mudtown,
William lets go of his father's refrain.
Whispers to Beauty, *We're almost there.*

They make their way
Among ghosts of early-blooming flowers
Gone to seed
Having left behind husks dry as the burrs that
Lurk along the sloping path to the Hilltop,
Attach themselves to his trouser cuffs.

Beauty whispers back to her friend,
I know.
She knows that when William returns
From The Hill that night
Alone
He will not recall having stepped on ripe berries
Fallen from beaks of sparrows and jays in flight,
Juice staining the soles of his shoes the color of ink.
Or of blood.

She knows that because he once followed the Gypsies home
William will remember how to sing away Sorrow
Whenever he recalls how his pistol caught the
Light on the top of The Hill.
A gift from the sun illuminates the bullet's course.
Assures a swift release from her fate.

Knows too, that when he has sung enough
To truly hear her final whisper,
Grandpa will never forget that
Beauty lives forever
In the hearts of those she has sent him to love.

II

MY MOTHER'S FAVORITE SONG WAS
DANCING IN THE DARK

I had forgotten how
My mother would dance
In the kitchen of my childhood
To music from the radio, late at night.
Twirl in the narrow space
Between cupboards and fridge on one side
Cupboards and stove on the other.
Double sink at the front beneath windows facing out
To the unpaved road showering dust
Through the screens with each passing car.

In a dream
I'm standing at the sink in the second floor kitchen
In the apartment where she lived after my father died,
Its window overlooking the backyard/clothesline.
My mother is out there.
She's alive, vibrant.
Her hair is black.
She's young.

A beautiful bird, almost black
Flies down to her
With a small bouquet of yellow roses in its beak.
She accepts.
Then the bird opens its wings
Etched with silver and gold
Envelops my mother in its embrace
And they dance.

CECELIA

I run my fingers through my hair
Back on one side
Then the other.
An unconscious gesture until I remember
How I would watch her
Raising her arm
Slowly, with effort
Placing her fingers alongside her head
Then brushing them through the waves in her hair.
My hands are like hers
Not in their deformity
But like hers in family
Bloodline, in kinship.
They called her a cripple
But she was a woman
With the heart and the mind of a child.
She was willful and spoiled
She was quick. She was bright
And could walk, if there was someone to take hold of her arm
Or if she held on to the edge of the long oak table
As she shuffled her feet to the other side.
Most of the time though
She sat by the window
Perched on the faded wine velvet cushion
While she waited for life to come passing by.

SLEEP-OVER WITH AUNT CEIL IN HER BEDROOM AT AUNT MAY'S

To reach Aunt Ceil's bedroom, first I had to
Walk past Aunt May's dining room
Side-board on the left, table on the right
Then Uncy's *National Geographic Magazines*
Shelved chronologically behind locked wood-
Framed, glass cupboard doors on
Both sides of the parlor archway.

Picture portraits of ancestral faces,
Eyes glaring from behind carved
Mahogany ovals and squares above the sapphire
Blue, stuffed velvet sofa,
Following me, as I entered the chill, dark hallway
That led to the bedrooms. Aunt May's on the right.
Aunt Ceil's at the end.

The bed was soft.
The room was cold.

Aunt Ceil slept unaware as
Intermittent light from cars
Passed below on Oak Street
Entered the lowered,
Flimsy, canvas window shades.

While I lay awake
Witnessing the spirits of her
Favorite saints
Rise life-sized
Out of their porcelain bodies
Fly up
To envelop the Holy Pictures
Nailed on her
Floral papered walls.

TEREZA AND THE UNANSWERED QUESTIONS—
Especially the ones about her shoes

My grandmother's best friend, Tereza
Walked barefoot everywhere there was to go
Even in winter
Through drifts of snow that rose
Up from the earth in the Chapel Yard
Like mounds of meringue on a huge lemon pie.
Everyone knew her by name.

Some neighbors thought Tereza was crazy.
I think they secretly wished they could be like her.
Can you imagine what it must feel like to
Walk without shoes without stockings no
Laces to tie no
Heels to bend sideways get
Caught in a crack in the sidewalk
And break?
Nothing to come between you and your path,
Intuited by the soles of your feet?

How many lives did Tereza touch
Miles did she travel in roundabout ways?
Nothing linear occurred in my old, Italian neighborhood.
Thoughts?   Conversations?
Never linear.
The progression of time?
Be Serious!

And yet, there had to have been a time when Tereza wore shoes.
Not even my grandmother knew how to answer
Whenever I asked what had happened to make her stop.

Might whatever did happen
Occur on a mid-August morning before I was born?
Before Ann Caroccoia's roosters crowed
Proud to announce another hot, muggy day?
By afternoon, the air so full of moisture
You could drink it with a straw.

Maybe as Tereza was dressing,
Old Lady Cilento's married daughter
Pounded on her kitchen screen door?
Come Quick!
My baby, Francesca!
The doctor's medicine! It's not working!
Tereza will know what to do.

Buttoning her freshly pressed, cotton housedress as it
Flapped against her thighs, outlining legs
Strong from a lifetime of hard work in her garden,
Her hair, still dark and coarse, twisted into a rope
Swinging against the small of her back,
Tereza gave no thought to her shoes as she
Ran past the Pear Tree
Cut across the Chapel Yard on her way to
Remove the curse of the Evil Eye.

If I saw Tereza today
Would I think she was crazy?

Would you?

SABATO JOHN'S SECOND WIFE

Antoinette sits in her rocking chair
Summer sounds, like fireflies
Flit up to her open window.
Next to the wine cellar
In the locked coal bin
Crickets sing.

Hushed by evening, neighbor's voices
Slip off freshly scrubbed front stoops.
From the corner barroom
A woman's high-pitched laugh
Lifts itself out of the stale air and smoke.
Finds its own way out the door.

Purple-blue night seeps between shingles
Of the three-story gray house across the wide courtyard.
Spills down the sides of that fortress.
Seals all the windows.
Fills in the space underneath each back door.

Antoinette's step-children and their
Children live there.
From back porches
They call out to each other in daylight.
Almost never do they call out to her.
Even when she rocks back and forth
On her porch, hands resting in her lap.

Many years after her husband had died
And the children she made with him were gone,
A loneliness she could not begin to measure
Came to Antoinette in the middle of the night.

She remembers waking up in her bed
Startled by a tap, tap at her door.
No one ascended her stairs anymore.

Trembling, she got up and put on her slippers.
Wrapped in her shawl, ears filled
With the beat of her heart,
She found her way in the moonlight.
Unlocked the lock
Opened the door. Just a crack.
Enough to let Loneliness in.

It moved about Antoinette's house
As if it belonged there.
Drank from her cup. Sat in her chair.
Climbed into her bed.
At last. Home.

Sometimes on the most ordinary days,
She might be outdoors
Watering tomatoes in her vegetable garden
Grateful for the after-suppertime sun
Unburdening her shoulders,
Lost in the scent of sweet basil,
Loneliness sneaks up behind her
Twines itself around her breast
Whispers it will never leave her.
She will never be alone.

201 OAK STREET

Her back pressed against the knotty pine parlor wall,
Its stain bubbled, cracked and darkened,
My mother asks what I think she should do.

"It's up to you, Ma.
Do you really want to return to this house?"
Do you really want to share it
with the ghost of your disapproving sister-in-law?

Aunt May's house,
Part of the family compound.
We lived there until I was five.

Late afternoon shadows
Move from under back porch eaves
Through spaces in the rusted wire fence
Surrounding the empty lot next to the main house,
Where once there was a beautiful garden.
I was never allowed to step inside.

The sun attempts entry through maples and oaks,
Their knotted branches heavy with leaves.
Thorny vines climb past broken trellises,
Tangle on telephone wires.

I follow my mother into the backyard,
Measuring stick in hand,
For the first time in forty-five years.

She talks with the couple next door.
Tells them she wants to move back.
Needs to be on one floor.
Malignant mass on her lung.
No symptoms. Never smoked.
Surgery. A year now.
Might have radiation. You never know.

201 OAK REVISITED

I stand on the small porch off the kitchen
Where I posed for the camera when I was four.
Dressed like a Gypsy.
Centered in the spotlight
Of an Indian Summer Sun.

Today, on this almost autumn day,
The sky is gray.
My arms crossed to ward off the chill,
I lean against the wobbly porch banister
Try to ignore the layers of paint
Peeling off the dry, splintered wood.
Off the siding, the floor.

Voices from inside—my sister's, my son's
Travel out through the kitchen screen door.
The two have come from their New England homes
To walk with my mother outside and inside
Retrace the steps she had taken the week before in
This house we call "Oak Street."

I remind them about the smell in the kitchen.
It disturbs me.
Not paint or glue.
It smells of disappointment. Of loss.

I hear my mother say,
"It doesn't matter. I can live with that."
I know it's a lie.
I know that my sister and son
Feel they must honor her need to return.

In that moment
I am struck by the reality. If
She moves back to Oak Street,
I am the one who lives closest.

I am the one who will sit with my mother
In these shrunken, airless rooms.
I am the one who will watch her disappear
Into their darkened walls.
I am the only one who will smell that smell.

I can't say what compels me when I
Make my way back
Stop at the first basement window.
Wipe off the grime. Press my forehead to the pane.
Shield my eyes with my hands.
Peer inside.

I pretend to be calm when I call my sister
Tell her to look in.
She recoils at the sight, and calls my son.
We take turns at the window, transfixed.

Trapped between the dusty glass
The tumble of tables and chairs locked up
Left behind over decades to warp in the damp—
A bird.
And its lifeless eyes.

III

IT WAS MORE THAN THE SMELL OF LAVA SOAP

The memory, neatly tucked away for years,
Came out for some air on an ordinary October day and
Startled me with its clarity.

There I sat in the rocking chair in Aunt May's kitchen.
I could see the huge coal stove that spat out loaves of bread and
Tins of rolls and countless vanilla cakes, without effort,
For as long as I could remember.
I was twelve and had seen a lot in my lifetime.

I watched, with the others, as Aunt May went about her rituals—
Stoking the stove, lifting the kettle, pouring, stirring.
Transforming bits of nothing into most delicious somethings.
The room was quiet.

And then it began, a high pitched
Sound that went through my body
Penetrating my ear drums permeating my heart
Exiting through my toes leaving only to return
Again and again.
I sat immobilized, not sure if I should be
Afraid or embarrassed or both.

The long, steady sound was coming from Aunt May.
I had never heard the likes of it in all my years.
But then her husband had never died before, and
The others had gone before I was born.

I tried to fathom my father's face.
Aunt May was his sister, maybe
He knew what it was all about.
But he sat in silence, like the rest.
Let her do what she had to do.

Many years later, I sat
In the dark in Aunt May' kitchen.
Told her it was finally over.
My father, the last to remain, had died.

She was tired by then, so she simply cried.

OLD WOMEN'S SHOES

Unbeatable fortresses.
Sturdy.
Enclosed.
They covered the feet of the women who
Lived for the giving.

All tied up and
Toned down.

Useful to hold in.
To hold on.

I dreamed one night of a field
Dusted in twilight.
Planted with rows and rows of old women's shoes.
Turned upside down.
Staked to the ground.
Glistening with frost.
Impaled
Among the tomatoes.

THE FINAL SAY

After decades of marital devotion
Aunt May doubtless sat, spine straight,
Across from the lawyer, waiting for the
Words in her husband's will she had
Every right to expect to hear.

When Disbelief left her alone that night
Did she lie sleepless in her bed
Wondering what it was she must do
Or did the answer appear unbidden,
Rise up like her bread dough
Ready for baking?

When she bent over the coal stove at dawn,
Gripping the hem of her apron, to
Lift the metal latch on the oven door?
Made the Sign of the Cross over the
Bread pans she shoved onto oven racks?

Or when she sat in her rocker and waited to
Slit at its center
Each perfectly crusted loaf
With the tip of her sharpest knife?
Steamy Aroma set free.

The plan might have entered her mind
When she prepared for herself what
Once was her late husband's favorite meal.
Twisted the chicken's neck,
Oblivious to its final squawk.
Feathery carcass still warm in her hand.

Regardless of how her solution arrived,
Past regret, she made the decision:
Dig him up.
Get him out of her family plot.
Let him rot in unsanctified ground.

IV

FOOD THAT IS MORE THAN FOOD

I lift the store-bought, roasted red peppers out of the
Clear plastic container. Place them in a shallow
Ceramic bowl the color of goldenrod.
My sister has searched all over to find them for me
To serve with home-made meatballs and pasta, fresh
Italian bread and red wine— the menu, a family tradition
On special occasions. She will join me and my son
My daughter-in-law, my two young granddaughters
Around the dining room table that once was our mother's,
To celebrate my sixty-seventh year.

"They're not like what we grew up with." I answer
When she asks about the peppers. I've begun adding
Organic garlic, finely chopped, a generous splash of Extra-
Virgin olive oil. "But I know they'll be fine."
I mix all three ingredients with our mother's favorite spoon.
Let them sit for a while to marry the flavors. Time enough:

Still warm September afternoon, the Trudge Up Third Street,
Home From Grade School. Nearly There. Wood smoke curls its way
Along the alley behind our house. Meets me in the Chapel Yard.
Unmistakable aroma diverts me to its source, peppers roasting on
Old Lady Semenza's make-shift wood stove near the entrance to
Her back yard garden. Around the stove sit neighborhood women,
Among them our mother—the youngest, and only one
Not dressed to mourn forever.

Blackened in spots but still vibrantly red and green,
The seeded harvest will rest, layered with cloves of garlic,
Starkly white, in sealed glass jars until served anointed with golden
Yellow olive oil sent from the Old Country, pressed from olives
Picked by hand from silver leafed trees Sun Blessed in
Groves, planted for us by our people
Before The Time of the Brigands.

...we travelled this way.
Gauged our distance by stories
and loved our children.
We taught them to love their births.
We told ourselves over and over
Again, 'we shall survive this way.'
                    Simon J. Ortiz

OLD STORIES

How different might our lives have been?
If in this valley scarred by the need, the
Greed for coal, we had been taught to
Love our births.
Flourish in our lives.
Run from death, like Elk
Chased by Mountain Lion.
Pacing, out-distancing
Until a welcome surrender.
Knowing that our stories would be told
over and over to embrace, to
Embolden all who came after us.
Surviving this way.
Oh!

Instead, we sat frozen like snowmen with coal eyes.
Never moving from the spot.
Calling out the names of those who left
over and over
As if from their graves
They could return to us
Our stories.
Surviving this way.
Oh!

Acknowledgments

Grateful acknowledgment is made to the following publications:

The Writer in All of Us, Virginia Country, Voices in Italian Americana, Coalseam: Poems from the Anthracite Region

Special thanks: Patricia Chelland Toraldo, Mary-Catherine Jones, Joseph Hurka, Craig Czury, and always Frank J. Palescondolo.

MAGGIE MARTIN, daughter of Margaret and William Chelland, was born in the coal country of Old Forge, Pennsylvania. As Poet-in-Residence at the Wilkes-Barre, Pennsylvania, VA Medical Center, Martin specialized in healing through poetry. Her work has been published in numerous literary journals and magazines, and often anthologized. Her poetry was recently nominated for a Pushcart Prize. She lives on the bank of the Contoocook River in the foothills of the White Mountains of southern New Hampshire, close to her granddaughters, Abby and Sophie.

www.ingramcontent.com/pod-product-compliance
Lightning Source LLC
Chambersburg PA
CBHW072041060426
42449CB00010BA/2379